Raggedy Ann

A Thank You, Please, and I Love You Book

By Norah Smaridge
Illustrated by June Goldsborough

GOLDEN PRESS
Western Publishing Company, Inc.
Racine, Wisconsin

GOLDEN, A GOLDEN BOOK®, and GOLDEN PRESS®
are trademarks of Western Publishing Company, Inc.

Seventh Printing, 1972

Ann fluffs up the pillow
and smooths out the sheet.
Her bed is not lumpy
or bumpy—
it's neat.
She tucks in the blanket
and puts on the spread.
No wonder the pup
loves to sleep on her bed.

Andy is picking up his toys.
His room will soon be neat.
Ann looks in and smiles and says,
"Why, Andy! What a treat!"
He puts away his shoes and shirt,
  a sweater, and some ties. . . .
When friends come in to play today,
  they won't believe their eyes!

Ann holds her puppy safely—
　　gently, but firmly, too.
She doesn't want to hurt him,
　　he's so very small and new.
When Andy brings the puppy's food,
Ann puts him down with care.
He tastes the food and finds it good—
　　and soon there's no more there!

Ann sometimes goes on shopping trips.
She likes that very much.
She knows that she may LOOK at things
    but never, never TOUCH.
The things in stores are all for sale;
    they are NOT meant for play—
    so, if she damaged anything,
    poor Ann would have to pay.

People are very happy
    to hear Andy on the phone
because he always says hello
    in such a friendly tone.
He calls his sister to the room
    if she is far away,
    or takes a message for her
    in a very grown-up way.

Here in the sandbox
  our Andy and Ann
  share all of their playthings
  the best way they can.
(To fight in the sandbox
  they know is not wise—
  unless you like sand
  in your mouth, ears, and eyes!)

Andy likes swinging high himself,
  and that's the reason why
  he pushes Ann so hard that soon
  she's way up in the sky!
But when poor Ann calls, "High enough!"
  and squeals for all she's worth,
  he slows her down again with care
  and brings her safe to earth.

When Ann falls down
and scrapes her knee,
Andy is very quick
to put a bandage on it—
with a kiss to make it stick.

Ann won't give Andy
  a piece of her candy—
  it's not that she's meaning to tease.
He wants it so badly
  she'd give him some gladly—
  but Andy forgot to say PLEASE.

When Ann comes running in from play,
    she always wipes her feet
    in case her shoes are dirty
    from the playground or the street.
It only takes a little time
    (but she is glad, I'm sure,
    she's not a caterpillar, with
    a DOZEN feet or more!).

Andy takes care to close the door
   as softly as a mouse,
   for then he knows he won't disturb
   the people in the house.
He never, never slams the door
   (for Ann just might take fright—
   and jump—and drop the chocolate cake
   she's baking for tonight!).

"My name is Andy," says Andy to Ann,
    and he shakes her hand like a gentleman.
"My name is Ann," says Ann with a smile,
    and she shakes his hand in a friendly style.
Andy and Ann know each other well.
They're very good friends, as you can tell,
    but now they're practicing what to do
    when they meet someone who is really new!

Andy unwraps his spaceship.
"Oh, thank you, Ann!" he cries.
"It's what I've always wanted—
    a really great surprise!
Let's fly away together
    for a visit to the moon.
We'll splashdown in the ocean
    and be home this afternoon!"

Ann's next in turn to pin the tail,
    but Andy's hesitating.
Ann wishes he would hurry,
    for she's getting tired of waiting!
She stands there very quietly, though,
    because she knows it's true
    that if you wait for others
    they will kindly wait for you.

Nobody hears the telephone,
nobody hears the door,
nobody hears the cat's meow
or Rover's sleepy snore.
Nobody hears the baby howl
because he wants his toys—
Raggedy Ann's new one-man band
is making TOO MUCH NOISE!

Ann doesn't want dear Andy
to slip and hurt his head,
or bump his nose,
or break his toes
and have to stay in bed.
She holds the chair quite steady,
for this will help him land
as smoothly as an astronaut—
with cookies in his hand!

Somebody spilled the milk today!
Ann quickly wipes it up.
She knows just who that someone was—
   and it was *not* the pup!
A spill is such a messy thing,
   but paper towels are handy,
   and Ann is *always* pleased to do
   a little chore for Andy.

Ann puts her boots on by herself.
(It's puddle-y in the street.)
Sometimes she tumbles over,
    but she gets them on her feet.
Of course, it takes her quite a time
    to fasten up her slicker,
    but when she's had more practice,
    she will be a whole lot quicker!

When Ann and Andy sit at meals,
  they never reach for food,
  or sprawl,
  or stick their elbows out.
They know it would be rude.
They sit up straight
  and pass the salt
  as grown-up people do,
  and, though they like dessert the best,
  they eat their spinach, too!

Ann wants to read a fairy tale,
  but Andy wants a scary tale,
  and yet they never disagree
  about which story it should be.
They choose in turn;
  that way it's fun.
(They read *two* tales instead of one!)

When time has come to go to bed,
Ann never starts to pout,
  or whine,
  or fuss,
  or drag her feet
  and wear her family out.
She kisses everyone good-night
  and tells the cat and pup,
"The sooner I go off to bed,
  the sooner I'll be up!"

"I'll give you a bear hug," says Andy to Ann,
and he hugs her and hugs her as tight as he can.
"I love you," says Ann, getting up on her toes,
and she gives him a kiss on the tip of his nose.
They are fond of each other, it's easy to see,
and the reason is simple as simple can be!
They use their good manners wherever they go,
and this makes them *very* nice people to know!